Graceful Drapes: A Journey into the World of Salwar Kameez

Welcome to "Graceful Drapes: A Journey into the World of Salwar Kameez," a captivating exploration of one of the most beloved and iconic ensembles in the world of fashion. Embark on a delightful journey through the rich history, diverse styles, and cultural significance of the Salwar Kameez, a traditional Indian attire that has captivated hearts and turned heads for centuries.

In this book, we delve into the captivating tale of the Salwar Kameez, uncovering its origins, evolution, and timeless allure. From its humble beginnings as a practical garment to its status as a symbol of grace and elegance, the Salwar Kameez has stood the test of time and continues to mesmerize fashion enthusiasts around the globe.

Join us as we explore the myriad styles, designs, and variations of the Salwar Kameez, each rooted in regional traditions and showcasing the artistic finesse of skilled artisans. From the regal charm of the Anarkali to the simplicity of the Punjabi suit, each variant tells a unique story, reflecting the rich cultural heritage of India.

Throughout this journey, we will also unravel the fascinating interplay of fabrics, colors, and embellishments that adorn the Salwar Kameez. From intricate embroidery to vibrant prints, each element adds depth and character to this resplendent ensemble. We will uncover the secrets behind the selection of fabrics, the significance of motifs, and the craftsmanship that goes into creating these mesmerizing pieces.

Beyond its aesthetic appeal, the Salwar Kameez holds great cultural significance, representing identity, tradition, and community. We will delve into the social and cultural contexts in which this attire is worn, exploring its role in celebrations, ceremonies, and daily life. Through this exploration, we will gain a deeper understanding of the values and customs that have shaped the fashion landscape of India.

Moreover, we will explore the adaptability and versatility of the Salwar Kameez, as it transcends boundaries and finds its place in modern fashion trends. From fusion wear to contemporary designs, this traditional attire continues to reinvent itself while staying true to its roots.

"Graceful Drapes: A Journey into the World of Salwar Kameez" invites you to embrace the beauty and charm of this timeless ensemble. Whether you are a fashion enthusiast, a lover of cultural heritage, or simply intrigued by the allure of traditional Indian attire, this book promises to take you on a mesmerizing journey of discovery.

So, join us as we unravel the threads of tradition, admire the artistry, and celebrate the enduring legacy of the Salwar Kameez. Get ready to be enchanted by the graceful drapes that have bewitched generations and continue to weave their magic in the world of fashion.

I. Introduction

- Definition and significance of Salwar Kameez
- Historical background and cultural context

II. Regional Variations

- Salwar Kameez styles in North India
- Salwar Kameez styles in South India
- Salwar Kameez styles in East India

- Salwar Kameez styles in West India

III. Design and Construction

- Types of Salwar
  - Patiala Salwar
  - Churidar Salwar
  - Palazzo Salwar
- Types of Kameez
  - Straight Kameez
  - Anarkali Kameez
  - A-line Kameez
- Dupatta Styles and Draping Techniques

IV. Fabrics and Embellishments

- Popular fabrics used in Salwar Kameez
- Embroidery and Embellishment Techniques
- Prints and Patterns

V. Occasion-specific Styles

- Casual and Everyday Wear
- Formal and Office Wear
- Party and Festive Wear
- Bridal Salwar Kameez

VI. Styling Tips and Accessories

- Choosing the Right Salwar Kameez for Body Types
- Matching Accessories and Jewelry
- Hairstyles and Makeup to Complement the Outfit

VII. Contemporary Adaptations and Fusion Wear

- Modern Interpretations of Salwar Kameez
- Fusion with Western and Ethnic Elements

VIII. Salwar Kameez in the Global Fashion Scene

- Influence of Salwar Kameez in International Fashion

- Celebrities and Influencers Sporting Salwar Kameez

IX. Cultural Significance and Identity

- Salwar Kameez as a Symbol of Tradition
- Empowerment and Expression through Salwar Kameez
- Cultural Appreciation versus Appropriation

X. Sustainability and Ethical Considerations

- Handloom and Sustainable Practices
- Supporting Artisans and Craftsmanship

XI. Salwar Kameez as a Reflection of Diversity

- Celebrating Regional Styles and Cultural Exchange
- Exploring Unique Design Elements

XII. Conclusion

- Recap of Key Insights and Takeaways
- Encouragement to Embrace and Preserve Salwar Kameez

Definition and significance of Salwar Kameez

Definition: The Salwar Kameez is a traditional two-piece ensemble worn by women in various parts of South Asia, including India, Pakistan, and Bangladesh. It consists of a loose-fitting tunic top called the "Kameez" and a matching or contrasting pair of pants known as the "Salwar" or "Patiala." The Kameez typically has a straight or A-line silhouette, while the Salwar is characterized by its relaxed and billowy fit.

Significance: The Salwar Kameez holds immense cultural and social significance in South Asian communities. It is not merely a garment but a symbol of tradition, identity, and heritage. The ensemble reflects the region's rich history, diverse culture, and timeless elegance.

The Salwar Kameez embodies the essence of modesty, offering women a comfortable yet stylish option for everyday wear, formal occasions, and celebrations. It strikes a balance between modesty and fashion, allowing women to express their personal style while adhering to cultural norms and traditions.

Beyond its cultural importance, the Salwar Kameez has gained popularity across the globe for its versatility and adaptability. Its timeless design and graceful drapes make it a favored choice for women of all ages and body types. It can be customized to suit individual preferences, with various necklines, sleeve lengths, and embellishments to add a touch of personal flair.

Moreover, the Salwar Kameez serves as a canvas for

intricate craftsmanship and artistic expression. Skilled artisans meticulously embroider, embellish, and print these ensembles, creating stunning patterns, motifs, and designs that showcase the region's rich textile heritage. From delicate handwork to exquisite zardozi, mirror work, and block printing, each Salwar Kameez tells a story through its intricate details.

The Salwar Kameez is not just a fashion statement but a symbol of community and shared experiences. It brings together women from different backgrounds, generations, and walks of life, fostering a sense of unity and pride in cultural heritage. It transcends geographical boundaries, creating a common thread that connects South Asian communities across the world.

In summary, the Salwar Kameez represents more than just a garment; it embodies the essence of tradition, identity, and elegance. It is a testament to the rich cultural heritage of South Asia and continues to captivate hearts with its timeless beauty and versatility. Whether worn for everyday occasions or special celebrations, the Salwar Kameez remains an integral part of the sartorial tapestry of the region, celebrated for its grace, charm, and enduring significance.

Historical background and cultural context

Historical Background: The Salwar Kameez has a long and illustrious history that can be traced back several centuries. Its origins can be found in the Mughal era, where it was introduced as a comfortable and practical attire for women in the royal courts of India. Over time, it evolved to become a popular choice among women across various social strata.

During the Mughal period, the Salwar Kameez was primarily worn by women in the North Indian region, particularly in the provinces of Punjab and Kashmir. It gained prominence as a traditional ensemble that reflected the cultural and social values of the time. The Mughal influence is evident in the intricate embroidery, rich fabrics, and regal designs that became synonymous with the Salwar Kameez.

Cultural Context: The Salwar Kameez holds immense cultural significance in South Asian societies, where it is deeply rooted in the region's traditions, customs, and way of life. It is considered a quintessential part of ethnic wear and is worn on various occasions, ranging from everyday routines to festive celebrations and formal events.

The Salwar Kameez reflects the cultural diversity of South Asia, with each region and community infusing its unique flavors into the ensemble. In India, for example, the traditional Punjabi style of the Salwar Kameez is known for its vibrant colors, bold prints, and voluminous Patiala pants. In contrast, the Lucknowi style from Uttar Pradesh is known for its delicate Chikankari embroidery and pastel hues.

In Pakistan, the Salwar Kameez is an integral part of the national dress and is worn by both men and women. The Pakistani style often features long, flowing silhouettes with intricate thread work, mirror work, and embellishments. Similarly, in Bangladesh, the Salwar Kameez is known as the "Shalwar Kameez" and is an essential part of the traditional attire, worn on religious and cultural occasions.

The Salwar Kameez not only showcases the aesthetics and craftsmanship of the region but also reflects the social, religious, and cultural values of the wearer. It is often worn as a symbol of modesty and respect, aligning with the cultural norms and customs of the respective communities.

Today, the Salwar Kameez continues to evolve with contemporary fashion trends while staying true to its traditional roots. Designers and artisans explore innovative techniques, fabrics, and motifs, creating a fusion of modern aesthetics with traditional craftsmanship. The Salwar Kameez remains a beloved attire that captures the essence of South Asian culture, connecting generations and celebrating the rich heritage of the region.

Salwar Kameez styles in North India

Salwar Kameez styles in North India: The region of North India is known for its diverse and vibrant culture, and this is beautifully reflected in the various styles of Salwar Kameez that have originated and thrived in this part of the country. Each style carries its unique charm, reflecting the local traditions, aesthetics, and craftsmanship.

1. Punjabi Salwar Kameez: The Punjabi style of Salwar Kameez is perhaps the most well-known and popular variant, not just in North India but also globally. It is characterized by its vibrant colors, bold prints, and voluminous pants called Patiala Salwar. The Kameez (tunic) is usually knee-length or slightly longer, and it is often paired with a contrasting or matching dupatta (scarf). The Punjabi Salwar Kameez exudes a lively and energetic vibe, making it perfect for festive occasions and celebrations.

2. Lucknowi Salwar Kameez: Originating from the city of Lucknow in Uttar Pradesh, the Lucknowi style of Salwar Kameez is renowned for its elegance and intricate Chikankari embroidery. Chikankari is a traditional form of embroidery that involves delicate white threadwork on pastel-hued fabrics like muslin, cotton, or georgette. The Kameez is typically long and flowing, with fine embroidery adorning the front, back, and sleeves. The Salwar (bottoms) are often made of sheer or lightweight fabric, adding to the overall grace of the ensemble.

3. Rajasthani Salwar Kameez: Rajasthan, known for its vibrant culture and rich heritage, offers a distinct

style of Salwar Kameez that showcases the region's royal aesthetics. The Rajasthani Salwar Kameez is characterized by its bright and vibrant colors, mirror work, and intricate embroidery. The Kameez is usually long and flowing, with embellishments adorning the yoke, sleeves, and hemline. The Salwar is typically a loose-fitting, comfortable bottom that complements the grandeur of the Kameez. This style is often worn during cultural festivities, weddings, and traditional events in Rajasthan.

4. Haryanvi Salwar Kameez: Haryana, another state in North India, has its unique style of Salwar Kameez. The Haryanvi Salwar Kameez is known for its simplicity and earthy tones. The Kameez is usually knee-length and features minimal embellishments or embroidery. The Salwar is typically a straight-cut or slightly flared bottom that offers ease of movement. This style reflects the rural traditions and the agrarian lifestyle of the region.

These are just a few examples of the diverse Salwar Kameez styles that can be found in North India. Each style carries its own charm and significance, representing the distinct cultural identity of the region. From the vibrant and lively Punjabi style to the intricate Chikankari of Lucknow and the royal grandeur of Rajasthan, the North Indian Salwar Kameez styles showcase the rich heritage and artistic traditions of the region.

Salwar Kameez styles in South India

Salwar Kameez styles in South India: The cultural diversity of India is beautifully reflected in the various regional styles of Salwar Kameez. When it comes to South India, the region offers its own unique interpretations and variations of this traditional attire. Let's explore some of the Salwar Kameez styles popular in South India:

1. Anarkali Salwar Kameez: The Anarkali style of Salwar Kameez is loved and widely worn in South India. It features a long, flared Kameez that flows gracefully, often reaching ankle-length. The Kameez is fitted around the bodice and then flares out from the waist, creating a regal and feminine silhouette. It is usually paired with a fitted Churidar (narrow-fitted bottoms) and a dupatta (scarf) to complete the ensemble. Anarkali Salwar Kameez is known for its intricate embroidery, rich fabrics, and vibrant colors, making it a popular choice for weddings, festivals, and special occasions.

2. Kerala Style Salwar Kameez: Kerala, known as "God's Own Country," has its distinctive style of Salwar Kameez that reflects the serene and elegant culture of the state. The Kerala style Salwar Kameez is characterized by its simplicity and minimalistic designs. The Kameez is typically long and straight, often made of soft and breathable fabrics like cotton or handloom. It is paired with a matching or contrasting bottom called Mundu, which is a two-piece drape worn around the waist. The ensemble is completed with a simple dupatta, if worn.

This style is favored for its comfort and understated elegance, making it suitable for casual wear and daily routines.

3. Tamil Nadu Style Salwar Kameez: Tamil Nadu, a state with a rich cultural heritage, showcases its own distinct style of Salwar Kameez. The Tamil Nadu style Salwar Kameez features a fitted Kameez that can be either short or knee-length. The bottoms are usually tight-fitting leggings called Churidar. This style is known for its vibrant colors, intricate handwoven designs, and temple-inspired motifs. The fabric choices include silk, cotton, and handloom textiles. It is often adorned with traditional jewelry and accessories, adding to its overall charm. The Tamil Nadu style Salwar Kameez is worn during festivals, cultural events, and special occasions.

These are some of the prominent Salwar Kameez styles found in South India. Each style carries its own cultural significance, reflecting the traditions and aesthetics of the region. From the grandeur of Anarkali to the simplicity of Kerala style and the intricate designs of Tamil Nadu, the Salwar Kameez styles in South India showcase the artistic diversity and richness of the region's heritage.

Salwar Kameez styles in East India

Salwar Kameez styles in East India: East India is known for its rich cultural heritage and exquisite craftsmanship, and this is beautifully reflected in the Salwar Kameez styles unique to the region. Let's explore some of the Salwar Kameez styles popular in East India:

1. Bengali Style Salwar Kameez: The Bengali style Salwar Kameez is known for its distinctive draping style and elegant designs. The Kameez is typically long, reaching below the knee, and is paired with a wide-legged bottom called a "Pajama" or "Palazzo." The draping style of the dupatta is also unique, with one end draped around the shoulders and the other end tucked in at the back. The Bengali style Salwar Kameez is often made from handloom fabrics like Tant, Jamdani, or Baluchari, featuring intricate weaving patterns and motifs. This style is worn during traditional Bengali occasions, festivals like Durga Puja, and weddings.

2. Odisha Style Salwar Kameez: Odisha, renowned for its handloom heritage, offers a distinct style of Salwar Kameez known for its intricate weaving and traditional motifs. The Kameez is usually knee-length and paired with a comfortable bottom called a "Pata." The highlight of the Odisha style Salwar Kameez is the traditional Ikat weaving technique used to create geometric patterns and vibrant colors. The fabric choices include Sambalpuri cotton, silk, or Tussar silk. The ensemble is completed with a matching or contrasting dupatta. This style is favored for its craftsmanship and traditional

charm, making it suitable for festivals, cultural events, and formal occasions.

3. Assamese Style Salwar Kameez: The Assamese style Salwar Kameez is known for its simplicity and elegance. The Kameez is typically long and loose-fitting, made from handwoven Muga silk or cotton fabric. It is paired with a wrap-around skirt called a "Mekhela" and a matching or contrasting dupatta. The Mekhela is draped around the waist, creating pleats in the front, and the loose end is wrapped around the body. The Assamese style Salwar Kameez often features intricate motifs inspired by nature, wildlife, and traditional Assamese designs. It is worn during festivals, weddings, and cultural celebrations in Assam.

These are some of the prominent Salwar Kameez styles found in East India. Each style carries its own unique characteristics and represents the cultural heritage of the region. Whether it's the elegant drapes of Bengali style, the intricate weaves of Odisha style, or the simplicity of Assamese style, Salwar Kameez in East India reflects the artistic traditions and cultural diversity of the region.

Salwar Kameez styles in West India

Salwar Kameez styles in West India: West India is known for its vibrant and diverse culture, and the Salwar Kameez styles in this region reflect the unique heritage and fashion sensibilities of the states. Let's explore some popular Salwar Kameez styles in West India:

1. Gujarati Style Salwar Kameez: The Gujarati style Salwar Kameez is characterized by its vibrant colors, intricate mirror work, and embellishments. The Kameez is typically long, often reaching below the knee, and is paired with a loose-fitting bottom called a "Churidar" or "Patiala." The Kameez is adorned with mirror work, embroidery, and colorful patchwork, creating a visually stunning ensemble. The dupatta is draped in various styles, with one of the most common being the "Seedha Pallu" style, where the dupatta is draped across the shoulder and pinned on one side. This style of Salwar Kameez is worn during festivals, weddings, and other celebratory occasions in Gujarat.

2. Rajasthani Style Salwar Kameez: The Rajasthani style Salwar Kameez reflects the royal heritage and rich cultural traditions of Rajasthan. The Kameez is usually long and adorned with intricate embroidery, mirror work, and bandhani (tie-dye) patterns. It is paired with a wide-legged bottom called a "Bajirao," which provides ease of movement. The ensemble is completed with a colorful and embellished dupatta. The Rajasthani style Salwar Kameez is often made from traditional fabrics like silk, chiffon, or georgette, showcasing the vibrant

colors and artistic craftsmanship of the region. It is worn during festivals, weddings, and cultural events in Rajasthan.

3. Maharashtrian Style Salwar Kameez: The Maharashtrian style Salwar Kameez, also known as the "Kurta-Pajama," is characterized by its simplicity and elegance. The Kameez is typically knee-length or slightly longer and is paired with a straight-cut bottom called a "Pajama." The Kameez is usually made from handloom fabrics like cotton or silk and may feature minimal embellishments or embroidery. The ensemble is completed with a traditional Maharashtrian-style waistband called a "Nauvari" or "Dhoti." The Maharashtrian style Salwar Kameez is commonly worn during traditional Maharashtrian festivals, cultural events, and religious ceremonies.

These are some of the prominent Salwar Kameez styles found in West India. Each style reflects the unique cultural identity and fashion aesthetics of the region. Whether it's the vibrant Gujarati style, the royal Rajasthani style, or the elegant Maharashtrian style, Salwar Kameez in West India is a symbol of tradition, grace, and sartorial excellence.

Patiala Salwar

Patiala Salwar: Patiala Salwar is a distinctive style of bottoms or pants that are commonly paired with Salwar Kameez outfits, particularly in Punjab and North India. The Patiala Salwar is known for its voluminous and pleated design, offering a relaxed and comfortable fit while exuding a regal and traditional charm. Let's delve into the details of Patiala Salwar:

1. Design and Features: The Patiala Salwar is characterized by its baggy and billowing silhouette. It features numerous pleats gathered at the waistband, creating a full and flared look. The pleats are typically stitched together at the bottom to maintain their shape. The Patiala Salwar is usually longer in length, extending up to the ankle or slightly below.

2. Draping Style: To wear a Patiala Salwar, one needs to gather the pleats around the waist, securing them with a drawstring or elastic. The gathered fabric creates a unique, layered effect that adds volume and movement to the outfit. The loose and relaxed fit of the Patiala Salwar allows for ease of movement and adds a touch of grace to the overall look.

3. Fabric and Embellishments: Patiala Salwars are crafted from a variety of fabrics, ranging from cotton and silk to georgette and chiffon. The choice of fabric depends on the occasion and personal preference. Traditional Patiala Salwars may feature intricate embroidery, mirror work, or embellishments at the hemline or along the pleats, adding a touch of glamour to the ensemble.

4. Versatility: The Patiala Salwar is highly versatile and

can be paired with various upper garments like Kurtis, Salwar Kameez, or even modern tops. It can be worn for both casual and festive occasions, offering comfort and a traditional yet stylish appeal. The Patiala Salwar is particularly popular during festivals, weddings, and cultural celebrations in Punjab and North India.

The Patiala Salwar is a beloved style that represents the cultural heritage and fashion traditions of Punjab. It is admired for its distinctive silhouette, comfort, and the graceful way it drapes around the body. Whether worn as part of a traditional Salwar Kameez ensemble or paired with modern tops, the Patiala Salwar adds a touch of elegance and regality to any outfit.

Churidar Salwar

Churidar Salwar: Churidar Salwar is a classic style of bottoms or pants that complements the elegance of Salwar Kameez outfits. It is known for its sleek and tapered design, which enhances the overall look of the ensemble. Let's explore the features and significance of Churidar Salwar:

1. Design and Features: The Churidar Salwar is characterized by its long and fitted design that gradually tapers down the leg. Unlike other salwar styles, the Churidar is skintight from the waist to the knee and then flares out slightly towards the ankle. It is usually longer in length, reaching the ankle or even draping over the foot.

2. Unique Construction: What sets the Churidar Salwar apart is its distinctive construction. The fabric used for Churidar Salwar is cut in a way that it creates numerous vertical pleats or folds along the length of the leg. These pleats, when worn, create a bunched or wrinkled appearance around the ankles, resembling the pleats of a churidar, which gives the style its name.

3. Draping Style: To wear Churidar Salwar, one needs to gather the excess fabric at the ankle and create even pleats around it. The pleats are then tucked into the ankle or secured with a band, giving the Salwar a clean and tapered look. This style of draping creates a flattering and slimming effect, accentuating the curves of the legs.

4. Fabric and Embellishments: Churidar Salwars are made from various fabrics, including cotton, silk, georgette,

and crepe. The choice of fabric depends on the occasion and personal preference. Churidar Salwars can be plain, allowing the focus to remain on the intricacy of the accompanying Kameez, or they can be embellished with decorative elements such as lace, embroidery, or sequins.

5. Versatility: Churidar Salwar is a versatile bottom wear option that complements various styles of tops and tunics. It can be paired with short or long Kameez, Kurtis, or even Indo-western tops, making it suitable for both casual and formal occasions. The sleek and tapered design of Churidar Salwar adds a touch of sophistication to any outfit.

Churidar Salwar is a popular choice among women for its elegant and figure-flattering appeal. Its sleek and tapered design, along with the unique construction of vertical pleats, creates a distinctive look that enhances the overall aesthetic of Salwar Kameez ensembles. Whether worn for everyday wear, festive occasions, or special events, Churidar Salwar adds a touch of grace and sophistication to traditional Indian attire.

Palazzo Salwar

Palazzo Salwar: Palazzo Salwar is a stylish and contemporary variation of bottoms or pants that has gained popularity in recent years. It offers a comfortable and chic alternative to traditional Salwar Kameez outfits. Let's explore the features and significance of Palazzo Salwar:

1. Design and Features: Palazzo Salwar is characterized by its wide-legged, loose-fitting design. It features wide and flowing pants that start from the waist and extend down to the ankle. The pants have a relaxed and breezy silhouette, offering freedom of movement and a modern, bohemian aesthetic.

2. Comfort and Versatility: Palazzo Salwar is known for its comfort and ease of wear. The wide-legged design allows for ample airflow and unrestricted movement, making it suitable for various occasions and climates. It can be worn casually for everyday activities, as well as dressed up for formal events, depending on the fabric and embellishments used.

3. Fabric and Embellishments: Palazzo Salwars are made from a variety of fabrics, including cotton, silk, chiffon, georgette, and crepe. The choice of fabric determines the drape and overall look of the pants. Palazzo Salwars can be plain and simple, allowing the focus to remain on the upper garment, or they can feature embellishments such as prints, embroidery, sequins, or lace, adding a touch of glamour to the outfit.

4. Styling Options: Palazzo Salwar offers endless styling possibilities. It can be paired with short or long Kameez,

Kurtis, tunics, or even crop tops, depending on the desired look and occasion. The loose and flowing nature of Palazzo Salwar creates a relaxed and effortless vibe, making it a popular choice for casual outings, parties, and even weddings.

5. Contemporary Appeal: Palazzo Salwar has gained popularity due to its modern and fashion-forward appeal. It combines the comfort of traditional Indian attire with the contemporary aesthetics of wide-legged pants. The versatile and trendy nature of Palazzo Salwar has made it a favorite among women of all ages and has become a staple in many wardrobes.

Palazzo Salwar offers a fresh and stylish twist to traditional Indian attire. With its wide-legged design, comfortable fit, and versatile styling options, it has become a go-to choice for women looking for both fashion and comfort. Whether worn for casual occasions, festive celebrations, or formal events, Palazzo Salwar adds a touch of contemporary elegance to any outfit, making it a must-have in the modern woman's wardrobe.

Straight Kameez

Straight Kameez: The Straight Kameez is a classic and timeless style of the upper garment in a Salwar Kameez ensemble. Known for its elegant and straight silhouette, the Straight Kameez offers a sophisticated and graceful look. Let's explore the features and significance of the Straight Kameez:

1. Design and Features: The Straight Kameez is characterized by its straight and fitted silhouette, which falls gracefully from the shoulders to the desired length. It is typically knee-length or longer, depending on personal preference and occasion. The Kameez is designed to enhance the body's natural contours while maintaining a modest and dignified appearance.

2. Versatility and Adaptability: The Straight Kameez is incredibly versatile and can be styled in various ways to suit different occasions and personal preferences. It can be paired with different bottom styles such as Churidar, Salwar, Palazzo, or even skirts, allowing for endless styling possibilities. The simplicity of its design makes it adaptable to both casual and formal settings.

3. Fabrics and Embellishments: The Straight Kameez is crafted from a wide range of fabrics, including cotton, silk, georgette, chiffon, and more. The choice of fabric can determine the drape and overall look of the garment. The Straight Kameez can be kept simple and minimalistic, highlighting the beauty of the fabric itself, or it can be adorned with various embellishments such as embroidery, sequins, beads, or prints, adding a touch of elegance and glamour.

4. Cultural Significance: The Straight Kameez holds cultural significance and is deeply rooted in the traditional attire of many regions in India. It reflects the timeless grace and femininity of Indian women. The Straight Kameez is not only worn for daily wear but also for special occasions, festivals, and celebrations. It symbolizes the rich cultural heritage and diverse traditions of India.

5. Styling Options: The Straight Kameez offers a wide range of styling options. It can be paired with different types of bottoms, such as traditional Salwar, Churidar, or modern Palazzo pants, to create various looks. It can also be accessorized with statement jewelry, scarves, or dupattas to enhance the overall outfit. The Straight Kameez allows women to express their personal style while embracing the elegance and grace of traditional Indian attire.

The Straight Kameez is a classic and versatile garment that exudes grace and sophistication. Its timeless design and cultural significance make it a popular choice among women of all ages. Whether worn for daily wear, festive occasions, or formal events, the Straight Kameez offers a perfect blend of tradition and contemporary style. With its clean lines, flattering fit, and endless styling possibilities, it continues to be a cherished and beloved attire in the rich tapestry of Indian fashion.

Anarkali Kameez

Anarkali Kameez: The Anarkali Kameez is a stunning and regal style of the upper garment in a Salwar Kameez ensemble. Known for its flared silhouette and intricate embellishments, the Anarkali Kameez captivates with its timeless elegance. Let's delve into the features and significance of the Anarkali Kameez:

1. Flared Silhouette: The Anarkali Kameez is characterized by its voluminous and flowing silhouette. The Kameez flares out from the waist or hips in multiple tiers or panels, creating a graceful and princess-like effect. The flared design adds movement and drama to the outfit, making it a perfect choice for special occasions and celebrations.

2. Elaborate Embellishments: The Anarkali Kameez is known for its exquisite embellishments and intricate craftsmanship. It is often adorned with intricate embroidery, zari work, sequins, beads, and other decorative elements. These embellishments can be found on the bodice, sleeves, and hemline of the Kameez, creating a stunning visual appeal and adding a touch of opulence to the ensemble.

3. Length and Style Variations: The Anarkali Kameez comes in various lengths, ranging from knee-length to floor-length. The longer versions are often referred to as "floor-length Anarkalis" and are favored for formal occasions and bridal wear. The style variations include sleeveless, full sleeves, cap sleeves, or even off-shoulder styles, allowing women to choose a design that complements their personal style and preferences.

4. Rich Fabrics: The Anarkali Kameez is crafted from a variety of luxurious fabrics such as silk, velvet, georgette, chiffon, or net. These fabrics lend a rich and royal touch to the garment, enhancing its overall appeal. The choice of fabric can also influence the drape and movement of the Anarkali, creating a graceful and flowing effect.

5. Cultural Significance: The Anarkali Kameez finds its roots in the Mughal era, reflecting the grandeur and splendor of that time. It is named after the legendary courtesan Anarkali, known for her beauty and elegance. The Anarkali Kameez symbolizes a blend of Mughal and Indian cultural influences, showcasing a fusion of styles and craftsmanship.

6. Occasions and Celebrations: The Anarkali Kameez is commonly worn for weddings, festive occasions, parties, and other grand celebrations. Its royal and regal appearance makes it a popular choice for brides, bridesmaids, and women who want to make a statement at special events. The Anarkali Kameez exudes grace, sophistication, and femininity, making it an ideal choice for those seeking a glamorous and timeless look.

The Anarkali Kameez is a masterpiece of traditional Indian attire, capturing the essence of royal elegance and opulence. Its flared silhouette, intricate embellishments, and rich fabrics create a mesmerizing and captivating ensemble. Whether worn by a bride on her wedding day or by a woman attending a festive gathering, the Anarkali Kameez brings forth a sense of grace, beauty, and cultural heritage. It continues to be a beloved and cherished attire, transcending time and trends with its timeless appeal.

A-line Kameez

A-line Kameez: The A-line Kameez is a classic and versatile style of the upper garment in a Salwar Kameez ensemble. Known for its clean lines and flattering silhouette, the A-line Kameez offers a perfect blend of elegance and comfort. Let's explore the features and significance of the A-line Kameez:

1. Silhouette: The A-line Kameez gets its name from its distinctive A-shaped silhouette. It is fitted at the top and gradually widens towards the hem, resembling the shape of the letter "A." This design feature makes the A-line Kameez universally flattering and suitable for various body types. The A-line silhouette provides a balanced and graceful look while offering ease of movement.

2. Tailoring and Structure: The A-line Kameez is well-structured and tailored to accentuate the natural curves of the body. It is fitted at the bust and waist, highlighting the feminine figure, and then flows gently down without clinging to the body. This style offers a comfortable and relaxed fit, allowing for easy mobility.

3. Length and Hemline: The A-line Kameez comes in different lengths, ranging from knee-length to ankle-length. The hemline is typically straight or slightly flared, maintaining the A-line shape. The length can be chosen based on personal preference and the occasion. Knee-length A-line Kameez is suitable for casual and everyday wear, while ankle-length A-line Kameez is often preferred for more formal occasions.

4. Versatility: The A-line Kameez is highly versatile and

can be styled in various ways to suit different occasions and personal preferences. It can be paired with different types of bottom wear, such as churidar, salwar, or even palazzo pants, to create different looks. The simplicity of the A-line silhouette allows for experimentation with accessories, layering, and mix-and-match options.

5. Fabrics and Embellishments: The A-line Kameez can be crafted from a wide range of fabrics, including cotton, silk, georgette, chiffon, and more. The choice of fabric depends on the desired look and the occasion. A-line Kameez can be adorned with minimal embellishments for a casual or everyday look, while for more formal occasions, it can feature intricate embroidery, sequins, or other decorative elements.

6. Occasions and Wearability: The A-line Kameez is suitable for a variety of occasions, from casual gatherings to formal events. Its versatile nature makes it an ideal choice for both day and evening wear. The simplicity of the design makes it a popular option for office wear, while the addition of embellishments and rich fabrics can elevate it to a more festive or celebratory outfit.

The A-line Kameez is a timeless and effortlessly elegant style that has been embraced by women for its flattering silhouette and versatility. Its clean lines, comfortable fit, and adaptability to different occasions make it a wardrobe staple for many. Whether worn with traditional bottom wear or fused with contemporary elements, the A-line Kameez is a symbol of grace and sophistication, embodying the essence of traditional Indian attire.

Dupatta Styles and Draping Techniques

Dupatta Styles and Draping Techniques: The dupatta is an integral part of a traditional Salwar Kameez ensemble, adding beauty, elegance, and versatility to the overall look. It is a long, rectangular piece of fabric that can be styled in various ways to complement the Salwar Kameez. Let's explore some popular dupatta styles and draping techniques:

1. Basic Over-the-Shoulder Drape: This is the most common and simple way of draping the dupatta. The dupatta is placed over one shoulder and draped across the chest, allowing it to fall gracefully over the opposite arm. This style is easy to achieve and is suitable for both casual and formal occasions.

2. One-Sided Dupatta Drape: In this style, the dupatta is draped over one shoulder and brought across the front diagonally to be pleated and tucked into the side of the Salwar or waistband. This draping technique adds a touch of elegance and can be enhanced with embellishments or decorative pins.

3. Double Dupatta Drape: For a more elaborate and regal look, two dupattas can be worn. The first dupatta is draped over the shoulder as described in the previous styles, while the second dupatta is draped diagonally across the other shoulder, creating a beautiful layered effect. This style is often seen in wedding attire and adds a luxurious and traditional touch.

4. Side Sling Dupatta: This draping technique involves taking one end of the dupatta and slinging it across the chest, securing it on the opposite shoulder. The

remaining portion of the dupatta can be left hanging or pleated and tucked into the waistband. This style adds a contemporary twist and is popular for its asymmetrical and eye-catching look.

5. Lehenga Style Dupatta: Inspired by traditional lehenga choli draping, this style involves pleating the dupatta and securing it on one shoulder while allowing the remaining fabric to flow down the opposite arm or side. This style gives a royal and grand appearance, making it suitable for special occasions and wedding wear.

6. Head Dupatta Drape: In certain regions and for specific occasions, the dupatta is draped over the head as a sign of respect and modesty. It can be draped to cover the head entirely or partially, depending on cultural traditions and personal preference. This style adds a traditional and graceful touch to the overall look.

When draping the dupatta, it is important to consider the fabric, embellishments, and the overall aesthetic of the Salwar Kameez. The draping technique should complement the outfit, enhance the wearer's features, and provide comfort and ease of movement. Additionally, the dupatta can be adorned with tassels, borders, or decorative pins to add further elegance and flair.

The choice of dupatta style and draping technique allows individuals to express their personal style and creativity while honoring the cultural significance of the attire. Each draping style has its own charm and can transform the overall look of the Salwar Kameez, making it a unique and distinctive ensemble. Whether traditional or contemporary, the way the dupatta is draped adds a touch of grace and completes the essence of the Salwar Kameez ensemble.

Popular fabrics used in Salwar Kameez

Salwar Kameez is crafted using a wide range of fabrics, each with its unique characteristics, textures, and appearances. The choice of fabric plays a crucial role in determining the overall look, comfort, and durability of the Salwar Kameez. Here are some popular fabrics used in Salwar Kameez:

1. Cotton: Cotton is one of the most widely used fabrics in Salwar Kameez due to its breathability, comfort, and versatility. It is lightweight and suitable for everyday wear, especially in hot and humid climates. Cotton Salwar Kameez is known for its softness, ease of maintenance, and ability to absorb moisture.

2. Silk: Silk fabric adds a touch of luxury, elegance, and sheen to Salwar Kameez. It is a natural fabric known for its lustrous appearance and smooth texture. Silk Salwar Kameez is popular for special occasions and festivities, offering a rich and regal look. Varieties like Banarasi silk, Kanjivaram silk, and Tussar silk are commonly used.

3. Chiffon: Chiffon is a lightweight and sheer fabric that adds a delicate and ethereal appeal to Salwar Kameez. It drapes beautifully and has a flowing quality, creating an elegant and feminine look. Chiffon Salwar Kameez is often adorned with intricate embroidery or embellishments, making it suitable for formal occasions.

4. Georgette: Georgette is another popular fabric choice for Salwar Kameez, known for its slightly textured surface and lightweight nature. It has a graceful drape and a subtle sheen, giving the Salwar Kameez a fluid and

flattering look. Georgette Salwar Kameez is commonly seen in both casual and formal settings.

5. Crepe: Crepe fabric is characterized by its crinkled texture and slightly crisp feel. It offers a sophisticated and elegant appearance to Salwar Kameez. Crepe Salwar Kameez drapes well, has a smooth finish, and is often preferred for its wrinkle-resistant properties.

6. Satin: Satin is a glossy and smooth fabric that adds a luxurious and glamorous touch to Salwar Kameez. It has a sleek appearance and a soft, silky feel. Satin Salwar Kameez is often chosen for formal and festive occasions, where a radiant and refined look is desired.

7. Velvet: Velvet is a plush and rich fabric that imparts a royal and opulent look to Salwar Kameez. It has a soft pile and a smooth, lustrous surface. Velvet Salwar Kameez is often adorned with intricate embroidery or embellishments, making it ideal for grand events and evening wear.

These are just a few examples of the fabrics used in crafting Salwar Kameez. Each fabric brings its own characteristics and aesthetic appeal to the ensemble, allowing individuals to choose based on their personal style, comfort preferences, and occasion. The selection of fabric greatly influences the draping, fit, and overall appearance of the Salwar Kameez, making it an essential element in creating a stunning and comfortable outfit.

Embroidery and Embellishment Techniques

Embroidery and embellishments play a significant role in enhancing the beauty and intricacy of Salwar Kameez. These techniques add a touch of glamour, elegance, and cultural richness to the ensemble. Here are some popular embroidery and embellishment techniques used in Salwar Kameez:

1. Zari work: Zari is a form of metallic thread embroidery that involves weaving thin threads of gold or silver onto the fabric. It creates intricate patterns, motifs, and borders, giving the Salwar Kameez a regal and ornate look. Zari work is commonly found in traditional and bridal wear Salwar Kameez.

2. Resham (Silk) embroidery: Resham embroidery involves the use of silk threads to create colorful and intricate designs on the fabric. It can be done in various stitches like the satin stitch, chain stitch, or the intricate Kashida embroidery. Resham embroidery adds vibrancy, texture, and a sense of artistry to the Salwar Kameez.

3. Mirror work: Mirror work, also known as shisha embroidery, involves the use of small mirrors (shisha) to create reflective accents on the fabric. It is commonly found in traditional and folk-inspired Salwar Kameez, particularly in regions like Gujarat and Rajasthan. Mirror work adds a playful and eye-catching element to the ensemble.

4. Sequin work: Sequins are small, shiny, disc-shaped embellishments that are stitched onto the fabric to create a sparkling effect. Sequin work is widely used in both traditional and contemporary Salwar Kameez

designs, adding glamour and catching the light beautifully.

5. Beadwork: Beadwork involves the use of small beads, pearls, or other decorative elements to create intricate designs on the fabric. Beads are sewn onto the fabric using needle and thread, often in patterns or motifs. Beadwork adds texture, dimension, and a touch of luxury to the Salwar Kameez.

6. Gota Patti: Gota Patti is a traditional Indian embroidery technique that originated in Rajasthan. It involves the use of narrow strips of gold or silver ribbons, known as gota, to create intricate patterns and designs on the fabric. Gota Patti work is characterized by its shiny, metallic appearance and is commonly used in festive and bridal wear Salwar Kameez.

7. Thread work: Thread work refers to embroidery done using colorful threads to create intricate patterns and designs. It can be done in various stitches like the satin stitch, chain stitch, or the popular Kantha embroidery. Thread work adds texture, vibrancy, and a traditional touch to the Salwar Kameez.

These are just a few examples of the embroidery and embellishment techniques used in Salwar Kameez. Each technique carries its own cultural significance, regional variations, and aesthetic appeal. The choice of embroidery and embellishment depends on personal preferences, occasion, and the desired look of the Salwar Kameez. These techniques showcase the artistry, craftsmanship, and attention to detail that make each Salwar Kameez a unique and stunning piece of wearable art.

Prints and Patterns

Prints and patterns are an integral part of Salwar Kameez, adding depth, character, and visual interest to the ensemble. They reflect the rich cultural heritage and artistic traditions of India. Here are some popular prints and patterns commonly seen in Salwar Kameez:

1. Floral Prints: Floral prints are timeless and widely loved. They feature delicate, intricate, or bold floral motifs in various sizes and arrangements. Floral prints add a touch of femininity, grace, and natural beauty to the Salwar Kameez.

2. Paisley (Mehndi) Prints: Paisley prints, also known as mehndi prints, are iconic and have a long-standing association with Indian textiles. They feature the teardrop-shaped motif that is intricately woven or printed onto the fabric. Paisley prints bring a sense of tradition, elegance, and cultural richness to the Salwar Kameez.

3. Geometric Prints: Geometric prints feature geometric shapes, lines, and patterns arranged in symmetrical or abstract designs. They can be bold, modern, or traditional, depending on the design and color scheme. Geometric prints add a contemporary and eye-catching element to the Salwar Kameez.

4. Abstract Prints: Abstract prints are artistic and expressive, often featuring unconventional shapes, forms, and colors. They can be vibrant, bold, or subtle, creating a unique and artistic look for the Salwar Kameez. Abstract prints offer a creative and

individualistic approach to fashion.

5. Tie-Dye (Bandhani) Prints: Tie-dye prints, also known as bandhani prints, are created by tying sections of the fabric with thread before dyeing it. This process results in beautiful and distinctive patterns, typically in vibrant colors. Tie-dye prints add a bohemian, playful, and ethnic charm to the Salwar Kameez.

6. Block Prints: Block prints are created using carved wooden blocks dipped in dye and stamped onto the fabric. They create repetitive patterns and motifs that can be simple or intricate. Block prints are known for their traditional appeal, rustic charm, and organic feel.

7. Digital Prints: Digital prints are contemporary and innovative, created using digital technology. They allow for intricate designs, vibrant colors, and realistic depictions of various motifs, including nature, animals, landscapes, and more. Digital prints offer versatility and the opportunity to showcase detailed artwork on the Salwar Kameez.

These are just a few examples of the diverse range of prints and patterns that can be found in Salwar Kameez. Each print carries its own cultural symbolism, aesthetic appeal, and regional significance. The choice of print or pattern depends on personal style, occasion, and desired look. Prints and patterns infuse the Salwar Kameez with personality, charm, and visual appeal, making it a standout attire in any setting.

Casual and Everyday Wear

Casual and everyday wear Salwar Kameez is designed to offer comfort, ease of movement, and a relaxed yet stylish look for daily activities. These outfits are versatile and can be worn for various occasions, including work, college, shopping, or simply going about daily errands. Here are some features and considerations for casual and everyday wear Salwar Kameez:

1. Fabric: Choose lightweight and breathable fabrics like cotton, linen, or blended fabrics that provide comfort and allow for easy airflow. These fabrics are ideal for daily wear, as they keep you cool and comfortable throughout the day.

2. Silhouette: Opt for relaxed and semi-fitted silhouettes that offer freedom of movement. Straight-cut or A-line Kameez with slightly loose or comfortable fittings are popular choices. Avoid overly structured or heavily embellished styles for casual wear.

3. Neckline and Sleeve Length: Depending on personal preference, opt for necklines that suit your style, such as round neck, V-neck, or boat neck. Choose sleeve lengths according to the weather and your comfort level, such as short sleeves, three-quarter sleeves, or full sleeves.

4. Prints and Colors: Casual Salwar Kameez can feature a range of prints and colors to add vibrancy and visual interest. Opt for playful, fun, or subtle prints like stripes, polka dots, checks, or small motifs. Pastel shades, earthy tones, or bright colors can be chosen based on personal preference and skin tone.

5. Bottoms: Pair your Kameez with comfortable bottoms

like straight pants, churidar, or palazzo pants. These bottoms offer ease of movement and can be adjusted based on personal style and comfort.

6. Dupatta: For a casual and effortless look, you can choose to skip the dupatta or opt for a lightweight and minimalistic one. If you prefer wearing a dupatta, choose fabrics like chiffon or cotton with minimal embellishments to keep it lightweight and easy to manage.
7. Accessories: Keep the accessories minimal and suitable for daily wear. Opt for simple earrings, a wristwatch, or a delicate necklace to enhance your overall look without overpowering it.
8. Footwear: Pair your casual Salwar Kameez with comfortable footwear such as sandals, flats, or juttis. Choose footwear that complements the style and colors of your outfit.

Casual and everyday wear Salwar Kameez offers the perfect balance of comfort and style, allowing you to effortlessly navigate your daily routine while looking fashionable and put-together. By selecting the right fabrics, prints, colors, and accessories, you can create a chic and comfortable ensemble that reflects your personal style and enhances your confidence.

Formal and Office Wear

Formal and office wear Salwar Kameez is designed to exude elegance, professionalism, and sophistication. These outfits are suitable for professional settings, business meetings, formal events, or any occasion that requires a polished and refined look. Here are some features and considerations for formal and office wear Salwar Kameez:

1. Fabric: Choose high-quality fabrics with a polished finish and a slightly more structured drape, such as silk, georgette, or crepe. These fabrics lend a luxurious and professional touch to the outfit and ensure a sophisticated appearance.

2. Silhouette: Opt for well-tailored and fitted silhouettes that enhance your body shape without being too tight. Straight-cut or slightly flared Kameez with defined waistlines are popular choices for formal wear. Avoid excessively loose or flowy styles to maintain a polished look.

3. Neckline and Sleeve Length: Choose necklines that are modest and appropriate for professional settings, such as boat neck, high neck, or collared neck. Opt for sleeves of medium to full length, which give a more formal and refined appearance.

4. Colors and Prints: Opt for solid colors or subtle prints that are not too bold or vibrant. Classic hues like black, navy, gray, beige, or pastel shades are ideal for formal wear. Consider sophisticated prints like floral motifs, geometric patterns, or subtle embroideries.

5. Bottoms: Pair your Kameez with well-fitted bottoms like

straight-cut pants or churidar. These bottoms should have a tailored look and fit neatly around the legs. Avoid excessively flared or wide-legged bottoms for a formal setting.

6. Dupatta: Depending on the formality of the occasion, you can choose to wear or skip the dupatta. If wearing a dupatta, opt for one that complements the outfit and adds a touch of elegance. Consider fabrics like chiffon or silk with minimal embellishments.

7. Accessories: Enhance your formal Salwar Kameez with sophisticated accessories that complement the outfit without overpowering it. Opt for subtle and minimalistic jewelry like pearl earrings, delicate bracelets, or a statement ring. A sleek handbag and a classic wristwatch can also complete the professional look.

8. Footwear: Choose closed-toe footwear like pumps, heels, or dressy flats in neutral or coordinating colors. Select footwear that is comfortable for long hours and matches the formality of the outfit.

Formal and office wear Salwar Kameez allows you to maintain a professional and polished look while incorporating the elegance and cultural heritage of Indian attire. By selecting the right fabrics, colors, silhouettes, and accessories, you can create a sophisticated ensemble that showcases your professionalism and personal style.

Party and Festive Wear

Party and festive wear Salwar Kameez is all about celebrating joyous occasions and embracing vibrant and eye-catching looks. These outfits are designed to make a statement, exude glamour, and showcase intricate craftsmanship. Whether it's a wedding, festival, or special event, here are some features and considerations for party and festive wear Salwar Kameez:

1. Fabrics: Choose rich and luxurious fabrics like silk, velvet, brocade, or satin to add a touch of opulence to your outfit. These fabrics drape beautifully and often feature intricate embellishments, embroidery, or metallic threads.

2. Silhouette: Opt for silhouettes that allow for movement and grace. Anarkali, flared, or layered Kameez styles are popular choices for a dramatic and glamorous look. Consider asymmetrical hemlines, floor-length designs, or high-low cuts to add flair to your ensemble.

3. Neckline and Sleeve Styles: Experiment with statement necklines like halter neck, sweetheart, or deep V-neck to enhance the glamour of your outfit. Play with different sleeve lengths, such as sleeveless, cap sleeves, or bell sleeves, to add variety and create visual interest.

4. Colors and Embellishments: Embrace bold and vibrant colors like royal blue, deep red, emerald green, or regal purple for a festive look. Explore embellishments like sequins, stones, zari work, mirror work, or intricate embroidery to create a dazzling effect. Mix and match different embellishments to create a unique and personalized ensemble.

5. Bottoms: Pair your Kameez with bottoms that complement the glamour of the outfit. Flared or voluminous skirts, shararas, or lehenga-style bottoms are popular choices for a festive look. These bottoms often feature intricate work or embellishments to match the Kameez.

6. Dupatta: A dupatta adds an extra element of elegance and grace to your party wear Salwar Kameez. Opt for a dupatta in a contrasting or coordinating color, adorned with sequins, embroidery, or other embellishments. Experiment with different draping styles to create a stunning visual impact.

7. Accessories: Complete your party look with statement jewelry that complements the outfit. Consider wearing chandelier earrings, statement necklaces, or stacked bangles. Choose accessories that match the color palette and embellishments of your outfit.

8. Footwear: Opt for embellished or metallic footwear like heels or sandals to elevate your party look. Choose footwear that is comfortable enough to dance and enjoy the festivities while adding an extra touch of glamour to your ensemble.

Party and festive wear Salwar Kameez allows you to showcase your personal style, embrace vibrant colors, and indulge in the beauty of intricate craftsmanship. These outfits are designed to make you feel glamorous, confident, and ready to celebrate special moments with style.

Bridal Salwar Kameez

Bridal Salwar Kameez is a beautiful and elegant choice for brides who want to embrace traditional Indian attire while adding a contemporary twist to their wedding ensemble. Bridal Salwar Kameez offers a unique and stylish alternative to the classic bridal lehenga or saree. Here are some key features and considerations for bridal Salwar Kameez:

1. Intricate Embroidery and Embellishments: Bridal Salwar Kameez is known for its exquisite embroidery and intricate embellishments. Traditional techniques like zari work, resham embroidery, sequins, beads, and stones are often used to create stunning patterns and designs. The embellishments are typically heavy and elaborate, adding a touch of opulence and grandeur to the outfit.

2. Luxurious Fabrics: Bridal Salwar Kameez is crafted using rich and luxurious fabrics that enhance the overall look and feel of the ensemble. Silk, velvet, brocade, and satin are popular choices for bridal wear as they drape beautifully and add a regal touch to the outfit.

3. Silhouette and Cuts: Bridal Salwar Kameez offers a variety of silhouettes and cuts to suit different preferences and body types. A-line, Anarkali, or straight-cut Kameez styles are commonly chosen for bridal wear. These styles often feature voluminous skirts, flared bottoms, or layered designs that create a majestic and glamorous look.

4. Dupatta: The dupatta plays a significant role in

bridal Salwar Kameez. It is often heavily embellished, featuring intricate embroidery, sequins, or stone work. The dupatta can be draped in different styles to add a touch of elegance and grace to the overall ensemble.

5. Color Palette: Bridal Salwar Kameez offers a wide range of color choices beyond the traditional red. Brides can experiment with shades of maroon, pink, gold, blue, or pastel hues to reflect their personal style and preferences. The color palette can be chosen to complement the overall wedding theme or cultural significance.

6. Customization and Personalization: Bridal Salwar Kameez can be customized and tailored to suit the bride's specific requirements and preferences. Brides can work closely with designers to select the fabric, embroidery patterns, color combinations, and overall design elements to create a unique and personalized bridal ensemble.

7. Accessories: Bridal Salwar Kameez can be complemented with exquisite jewelry and accessories. Brides often opt for statement pieces such as heavy necklaces, chokers, maang tikka, jhumkas, and bangles. The choice of jewelry should complement the embroidery and embellishments of the outfit while adding a touch of glamour and elegance.

8. Footwear: Bridal Salwar Kameez is typically paired with embellished or traditional footwear such as embroidered juttis or heels. The footwear should be comfortable yet stylish, allowing the bride to move and dance with ease during the wedding festivities.

Bridal Salwar Kameez offers a stunning and contemporary option for brides who want to showcase their personal style while embracing traditional Indian attire. With intricate embroidery, luxurious fabrics, and attention to detail, bridal Salwar Kameez creates a memorable and enchanting look for the bride on her special day.

Choosing the Right Salwar Kameez for Body Types

When it comes to choosing the right Salwar Kameez for your body type, it's important to consider styles that flatter your figure and enhance your best features. Here are some tips to help you select the perfect Salwar Kameez for different body types:

1. Pear-Shaped Body: If you have a pear-shaped body with wider hips and thighs, opt for Salwar Kameez styles that draw attention to your upper body. Choose A-line or straight-cut Kameez styles that flow away from the hips and create a balanced look. Pair it with a fitted or slightly flared Salwar to create a slimming effect.

2. Apple-Shaped Body: If you have an apple-shaped body with a fuller midsection and narrower hips, look for Salwar Kameez styles that create an illusion of a defined waistline. Choose Anarkali or empire-waist Kameez styles that flare out from the bust and flow down gracefully. Avoid fitted or tight-fitting Salwars and opt for slightly flared or palazzo-style bottoms.

3. Hourglass Body: If you have an hourglass body shape with well-defined curves, embrace styles that accentuate your curves. Opt for fitted or semi-fitted Kameez styles that highlight your waistline. Pair it with a well-tailored Churidar or slim-fit Salwar to maintain the balance. Avoid overly loose or boxy styles that may conceal your curves.

4. Straight/Rectangular Body: If you have a straight or rectangular body shape with minimal curves, consider

Salwar Kameez styles that create the illusion of curves and add dimension. Choose Kameez styles with detailing around the bust or waistline, such as pleats, gathers, or embellishments. Opt for flared or layered bottoms to add volume and create a more feminine silhouette.

5. Petite Body: If you have a petite frame, opt for Salwar Kameez styles that create an illusion of height and elongate your figure. Choose shorter Kameez lengths that end above the knee or mid-thigh to create the illusion of longer legs. Pair it with slim-fit or straight-cut Salwars to maintain a streamlined look. Avoid overwhelming prints or large motifs that may overpower your frame.

6. Tall Body: If you have a tall stature, embrace Salwar Kameez styles that showcase your height and create a graceful look. Experiment with different Kameez lengths, from knee-length to floor-length, depending on the occasion and personal preference. Wide-leg Palazzo Salwars or Churidars can complement your height and add a touch of elegance.

Remember, these are just general guidelines, and it's important to try different styles and silhouettes to find what works best for your body type and personal style. Ultimately, the key is to feel confident and comfortable in the Salwar Kameez you choose, as it will enhance your natural beauty and make you shine.

Matching Accessories and Jewelry

When it comes to accessorizing your Salwar Kameez, the right jewelry and accessories can elevate your look and add a touch of glamour. Here are some tips for matching accessories and jewelry with your Salwar Kameez:

1. Earrings: Earrings are an essential accessory that can enhance your facial features and complete your overall look. Choose earrings that complement the neckline of your Kameez. For a V-neck or sweetheart neckline, opt for dangler or chandelier earrings. If you have a high neck or collar-style Kameez, choose statement stud earrings or small hoops. Jhumkas, traditional Indian earrings, are a versatile choice that can complement various styles of Salwar Kameez.

2. Necklace: The choice of necklace depends on the neckline of your Kameez and the overall look you want to achieve. For a simple and elegant look, a delicate pendant necklace or a single-strand pearl necklace can work well. If you have a deep neckline, consider a statement necklace with intricate designs or layers of chains. For a traditional touch, a Kundan or Polki necklace can add a regal feel to your ensemble.

3. Bangles and Bracelets: Bangles and bracelets are popular accessories that can add a touch of elegance to your wrists. Consider wearing a set of matching bangles or mix and match different styles and colors to create a vibrant look. If you prefer a sleeker look, opt for a single statement bracelet or a delicate chain bracelet.

4. Anklets: Anklets are a beautiful accessory that can add a

subtle charm to your Salwar Kameez. Choose a delicate silver or gold anklet with small charms or beads to complement your footwear and complete your look. They are especially great for showcasing your footwear when wearing shorter Kameez lengths.

5. Handbags and Clutches: A stylish handbag or clutch can be a practical and fashionable accessory to carry your essentials. Choose a handbag or clutch that complements the color and style of your Salwar Kameez. Embroidered or embellished designs can add a touch of glamour, while solid-colored or textured bags can create a more sophisticated look.

6. Footwear: The choice of footwear can greatly impact the overall look of your Salwar Kameez. For a traditional touch, opt for juttis or mojaris, which are intricately embroidered and comfortable to wear. If you prefer a more contemporary look, sandals, heels, or wedges can be stylish options. Choose footwear that matches the color palette of your outfit and provides comfort for the occasion.

Remember to strike a balance with your accessories and jewelry. If your Salwar Kameez has intricate designs or heavy embellishments, opt for minimalistic jewelry to let the outfit shine. Conversely, if your outfit is simple, you can experiment with bold and statement pieces of jewelry to add drama and flair.

Ultimately, the choice of accessories and jewelry should reflect your personal style and enhance the beauty of your Salwar Kameez. Have fun experimenting with different combinations to create a look that is uniquely yours.

Hairstyles and Makeup to Complement the Outfit

Choosing the right hairstyle and makeup can enhance your overall look and complement your Salwar Kameez. Here are some hairstyle and makeup ideas to consider:

Hairstyles:

1. Loose Waves: Soft, loose waves can add a touch of elegance and femininity to your look. This versatile hairstyle works well with most Salwar Kameez styles and is suitable for both casual and formal occasions.

2. Braided Updo: A braided updo can create a sophisticated and polished look. You can opt for a classic French braid, a fishtail braid, or a braided bun. This hairstyle keeps your hair neatly in place and adds a touch of elegance to your ensemble.

3. Side-swept Curls: Side-swept curls create a romantic and glamorous look. Curl your hair and sweep it to one side for an effortlessly chic hairstyle. This style works well with open-neckline Kameez or one-shoulder styles.

4. Sleek Ponytail: A sleek and high ponytail can give a modern and sleek look to your outfit. This hairstyle is perfect for a contemporary and stylish Salwar Kameez ensemble.

5. Half-Up, Half-Down: The half-up, half-down hairstyle strikes a balance between an updo and leaving your hair down. You can create a half-up ponytail, half-up bun, or half-up braid, allowing you to showcase your hair while

keeping it partially secured.

Makeup:

1. Natural and Fresh: Opt for a natural and fresh makeup look to enhance your features without overpowering your Salwar Kameez. Use a lightweight foundation or BB cream, a neutral eyeshadow palette, a touch of mascara, and a nude or light pink lipstick for a subtle and elegant look.
2. Smoky Eyes: If you want to add drama and intensity to your makeup, consider a smoky eye look. Choose shades that complement your outfit, such as charcoal, bronze, or deep plum. Pair it with a nude or neutral lip color to balance the overall look.
3. Bold Lip: Make a statement by choosing a bold lip color that complements your Salwar Kameez. A vibrant red, deep berry, or bright coral can add a pop of color and create a focal point for your makeup.
4. Dewy Glow: Achieve a luminous and dewy complexion by using a hydrating foundation or tinted moisturizer, a cream highlighter on the high points of your face, and a touch of blush for a healthy flush of color. Finish with a glossy or sheer lip color for a fresh and youthful look.
5. Subtle Contouring: Enhance your facial features with subtle contouring. Use a matte bronzer to add definition to your cheekbones, temples, and jawline. Remember to blend well for a natural look that enhances your facial structure.

Remember to consider the occasion and your personal style when choosing your hairstyle and makeup. Experiment with different looks and find what makes you feel confident and beautiful. Ultimately, the goal is to create a harmonious and balanced look that complements your Salwar Kameez and highlights your natural beauty.

Modern Interpretations of Salwar Kameez

Salwar Kameez has undergone modern interpretations that cater to contemporary fashion trends and personal styles. Here are some modern adaptations and interpretations of Salwar Kameez:

1. Indo-Western Fusion: Many designers and fashion enthusiasts have merged elements of Western fashion with traditional Salwar Kameez to create unique fusion ensembles. This can include pairing a crop top or a trendy blouse with a flared or straight-cut pants, or incorporating Western-inspired silhouettes and cuts into the Kameez.

2. Contemporary Silhouettes: Designers have experimented with various silhouettes to give Salwar Kameez a modern twist. This includes asymmetrical hemlines, high-low designs, cape-style Kameez, peplum tops, and jacket-style Kameez. These contemporary silhouettes add a fashionable edge to traditional attire.

3. Play with Lengths: Experimenting with the lengths of the Kameez and pants can create a modern and stylish look. Opt for shorter Kameez paired with cigarette pants or palazzos for a trendy and chic appearance. Alternatively, go for floor-length Kameez or Anarkali styles for an elegant and glamorous look.

4. Bold Prints and Patterns: Incorporating bold prints, abstract designs, and geometric patterns can bring a contemporary feel to Salwar Kameez. Play with contrasting colors, graphic motifs, and digital prints to

make a fashion-forward statement.

5. Sheer and Cut-Out Details: Adding sheer panels, lace inserts, or cut-out details to the Kameez can add an element of modernity and allure. These details create a visually interesting and trendy look while maintaining the traditional essence of the ensemble.

6. Statement Sleeves: Statement sleeves have become a popular trend in contemporary Salwar Kameez designs. Bell sleeves, ruffled sleeves, bishop sleeves, and lantern sleeves can elevate the overall look and add a fashion-forward touch.

7. Unique Necklines: Experimenting with different necklines can bring a modern twist to Salwar Kameez. Off-shoulder, cold shoulder, halter neck, keyhole, and asymmetrical necklines are some options to consider, giving the outfit a fresh and contemporary appeal.

8. Mix and Match: Embrace the trend of mixing and matching different elements of Salwar Kameez. Pairing contrasting colors, textures, and fabrics can create an eclectic and modern look. For example, combining a printed Kameez with solid-colored pants or vice versa.

9. Minimalist Approach: Embracing minimalism in Salwar Kameez designs can create a clean and sophisticated look. Opt for monochromatic or neutral-toned ensembles with clean lines and minimal embellishments for a modern and timeless appearance.

10. Styling with Accessories: Accessorizing plays a crucial role in modern interpretations of Salwar Kameez. Experiment with statement belts, contemporary jewelry pieces, trendy footwear, and modern handbags to complete your look and add a fashionable touch.

Remember, the key to modern interpretations of Salwar Kameez is to strike a balance between traditional elements and contemporary aesthetics. These adaptations allow you to express your personal style while paying homage to the rich heritage of

VIKASH DABRIWAL

Salwar Kameez.

Fusion with Western and Ethnic Elements

Fusion wear that combines Western and ethnic elements has become increasingly popular in the fashion world. Here are some ways you can incorporate Western and ethnic influences into your attire:

1. Jacket over Salwar Kameez: Layering a stylish jacket or blazer over your Salwar Kameez instantly adds a Western touch to the outfit. Opt for a tailored blazer, denim jacket, or a statement jacket in a contrasting color or pattern. This adds a contemporary edge while keeping the traditional essence intact.

2. Crop Tops with Palazzos: Pairing a trendy crop top with wide-legged palazzo pants creates a fusion look that combines Western and ethnic elements. Choose a crop top with interesting patterns, prints, or embellishments that complement the color palette of your palazzos. This combination is youthful, stylish, and perfect for casual occasions.

3. Shirt-style Kurtas: Opt for a shirt-style Kurta that features a collared neckline, button-down front, and tailored fit. This fusion style blends the structure of a Western shirt with the elegance of a Kurta. Pair it with straight pants or jeans for a chic and contemporary look.

4. Dhoti Pants with Western Tops: Dhoti pants, with their draping and pleating, add a touch of ethnic charm. Pair them with a Western-style top like a crop top, off-shoulder blouse, or a fitted shirt. This fusion ensemble

combines the flowy and traditional dhoti pants with modern and trendy tops.

5. Saree with Western Blouse: Give a modern twist to your saree by pairing it with a Western-style blouse. Opt for a cropped or off-shoulder blouse, a lace-up design, or a blouse with unique sleeves. This fusion creates a striking balance between the traditional elegance of a saree and the contemporary appeal of a Western blouse.

6. Tunic Dress: A tunic dress combines the comfort of a tunic with the silhouette and length of a Western dress. Choose a tunic dress in vibrant colors, intricate prints, or with ethnic-inspired details. Pair it with leggings or tights for a complete fusion look that is versatile and easy to wear.

7. Accessorize with Western Elements: Incorporate Western accessories like statement belts, oversized sunglasses, trendy handbags, and chunky jewelry to complement your ethnic attire. These accessories add a contemporary flair to your overall look and enhance the fusion aesthetic.

Remember, the key to successfully blending Western and ethnic elements is to maintain a harmonious balance. Experiment with different combinations, colors, and textures to create a unique fusion style that reflects your personal taste and celebrates the beauty of both cultures.

Influence of Salwar Kameez in International Fashion

Salwar Kameez has made a significant impact in the international fashion scene, inspiring designers and captivating fashion enthusiasts around the world. Here are some ways in which Salwar Kameez has influenced international fashion:

1. Global Runways: Salwar Kameez has graced international runways, with designers incorporating elements of its design and draping techniques into their collections. The versatility and elegance of Salwar Kameez have been showcased in prestigious fashion weeks, bringing Indian fashion to the global stage.

2. Celebrity Endorsements: Renowned celebrities, both Indian and international, have embraced Salwar Kameez as a fashion statement. Their appearances in Salwar Kameez at red carpet events, award ceremonies, and film festivals have elevated its visibility and popularity across the globe.

3. Bollywood Influence: Bollywood films, known for their glamorous fashion, have played a significant role in popularizing Salwar Kameez worldwide. Bollywood actresses donning exquisite Salwar Kameez in movies and promotional events have made a lasting impression, influencing fashion choices and trends globally.

4. Cultural Exchanges: With the increasing exchange of cultures and the celebration of diversity, Salwar Kameez has found its way into the wardrobes of fashion enthusiasts outside of India. Its unique design, vibrant

colors, and rich heritage appeal to individuals looking to embrace and incorporate global fashion into their own style.

5. Fusion Fashion: The fusion of Western and ethnic elements has become a prominent trend in international fashion, and Salwar Kameez has been a key component in this fusion. Designers and fashion enthusiasts experiment with blending Salwar Kameez with Western silhouettes, fabrics, and accessories, creating unique and contemporary ensembles that cater to diverse fashion sensibilities.

6. Designer Collaborations: Indian designers collaborating with international fashion houses and brands have introduced Salwar Kameez to a wider audience. These collaborations have resulted in unique collections that combine the design aesthetics of both cultures, showcasing the versatility of Salwar Kameez and its ability to adapt to different fashion sensibilities.

7. Street Style: Salwar Kameez has also made its mark in street style fashion across various cities around the world. Fashion-forward individuals incorporate Salwar Kameez into their everyday looks, pairing it with modern accessories, footwear, and outerwear to create fashion-forward ensembles that merge traditional and contemporary elements.

The influence of Salwar Kameez in international fashion is a testament to its timeless appeal, versatility, and cultural significance. It continues to inspire designers, fashion enthusiasts, and individuals seeking to embrace diverse fashion influences from around the world.

Celebrities and Influencers Sporting Salwar Kameez

Salwar Kameez has garnered the attention of celebrities and influencers worldwide, who have embraced this elegant ensemble in their personal style. Here are some notable celebrities and influencers who have been spotted sporting Salwar Kameez:

1. Priyanka Chopra: The globally acclaimed Indian actress and former Miss World, Priyanka Chopra, has been seen donning Salwar Kameez at various events and red carpets. She effortlessly carries the traditional attire with grace and elegance, showcasing its timeless appeal.

2. Deepika Padukone: Another leading Bollywood actress, Deepika Padukone, has often been spotted wearing Salwar Kameez for both casual and formal occasions. Her fashion choices have influenced many, and her stylish interpretations of Salwar Kameez have gained immense popularity.

3. Sonam Kapoor: Known for her impeccable fashion sense, Sonam Kapoor has experimented with Salwar Kameez in unique and innovative ways. She has been seen wearing designer versions of Salwar Kameez, showcasing its versatility and ability to make a fashion statement.

4. Aishwarya Rai Bachchan: Aishwarya Rai Bachchan, a former Miss World and prominent Bollywood actress, has embraced Salwar Kameez as part of her wardrobe. Her ethereal appearances in intricately designed Salwar Kameez have captivated the fashion world.

5. Nabela Noor: A popular Bangladeshi-American YouTuber and influencer, Nabela Noor, has been vocal about her love for Salwar Kameez and South Asian fashion. She often shares her stylish interpretations of Salwar Kameez on social media, inspiring her followers to embrace their cultural heritage.

6. Aimee Song: A well-known fashion blogger and influencer, Aimee Song, has been seen incorporating Salwar Kameez into her fashion-forward looks. She seamlessly blends the traditional attire with modern elements, creating unique and eclectic ensembles.

7. Hijabi Influencers: Many hijabi influencers from around the world have embraced Salwar Kameez as part of their modest fashion choices. They showcase the versatility of Salwar Kameez in providing comfort, style, and modesty, appealing to a wide audience.

These celebrities and influencers have played a significant role in popularizing Salwar Kameez beyond cultural boundaries. Their stylish interpretations and fashion-forward approach have made Salwar Kameez a go-to choice for individuals looking to make a fashion statement while embracing cultural diversity.

Salwar Kameez as a Symbol of Tradition

Salwar Kameez holds deep cultural significance and serves as a symbol of tradition in many South Asian communities. It represents the rich heritage and customs of the region, reflecting the values, beliefs, and identity of the wearers. Here are some reasons why Salwar Kameez is regarded as a symbol of tradition:

1. Cultural Identity: Salwar Kameez is deeply rooted in the traditions and customs of South Asian countries like India, Pakistan, Bangladesh, and Afghanistan. It is an integral part of their cultural identity, representing the diverse ethnicities and regional heritage within these countries.

2. Historical Significance: Salwar Kameez has a long history that dates back centuries. It has evolved over time, influenced by various rulers, empires, and cultural exchanges. The attire has witnessed the passage of time, preserving and celebrating the traditional aesthetics of the region.

3. Connection to Festivals and Celebrations: Salwar Kameez is often worn during religious festivals, weddings, and other cultural celebrations. It is considered appropriate and respectful attire for these occasions, highlighting the deep-rooted traditions and customs associated with these events.

4. Craftsmanship and Handloom Tradition: Salwar Kameez showcases the skilled craftsmanship and intricate handiwork of artisans and weavers.

From delicate embroidery to exquisite prints and embellishments, it exemplifies the artistry and talent of traditional artisans, keeping alive the legacy of traditional crafts.

5. Family and Community Traditions: Salwar Kameez is often passed down through generations as heirlooms, symbolizing the continuation of family traditions and values. It holds sentimental value and connects individuals to their roots, fostering a sense of belonging and cultural pride.

6. Respect for Customs and Etiquette: Salwar Kameez is considered modest attire, adhering to cultural norms and customs that emphasize modesty and respect. It reflects the values of grace, elegance, and propriety, which are highly regarded in traditional societies.

7. Preservation of Traditional Textiles: Salwar Kameez provides a platform for the preservation and promotion of traditional textiles and handloom industries. By wearing and supporting these garments, individuals contribute to the sustainability and livelihoods of artisans and weavers involved in the production of traditional textiles.

Salwar Kameez serves as a visual representation of tradition, enabling individuals to embrace and express their cultural heritage. It is not just a garment but a testament to the rich legacy, customs, and values that are deeply ingrained in South Asian societies. By wearing Salwar Kameez, individuals celebrate their cultural identity and honor the traditions passed down to them, creating a connection to their roots and fostering a sense of pride in their heritage.

Empowerment and Expression through Salwar Kameez

Salwar Kameez is not just a garment but a powerful symbol of empowerment and self-expression for many individuals. It holds the potential to transcend societal norms and allows individuals to showcase their personality, creativity, and individuality. Here are some ways in which Salwar Kameez empowers and enables self-expression:

1. Freedom of Choice: Salwar Kameez offers a wide range of styles, designs, and colors, providing individuals with the freedom to choose what resonates with their personal style and preferences. It allows individuals to break free from rigid fashion norms and express themselves authentically.

2. Versatility: Salwar Kameez is a versatile ensemble that can be customized and styled in various ways. From different types of bottoms like salwar, churidar, or palazzo to different types of kameez, such as straight, Anarkali, or A-line, individuals can experiment and adapt the outfit to suit their body type and personal taste.

3. Cultural Identity: Salwar Kameez enables individuals to embrace and celebrate their cultural identity. It serves as a visual representation of one's heritage, allowing wearers to connect with their roots, honor their traditions, and showcase their cultural pride.

4. Body Positivity: Salwar Kameez accommodates diverse body types and sizes, providing comfort and confidence

to individuals of all shapes and proportions. It allows wearers to feel comfortable and beautiful in their own skin, promoting body positivity and self-acceptance.

5. Expression of Individuality: Through the choice of fabrics, colors, patterns, and embellishments, individuals can express their unique personality and style. Whether it's opting for bold and vibrant hues or subtle and elegant designs, Salwar Kameez becomes a canvas for self-expression, enabling individuals to stand out and make a statement.

6. Bridging Tradition and Modernity: Salwar Kameez seamlessly blends tradition with modern fashion sensibilities. It allows individuals to embrace their cultural heritage while incorporating contemporary elements and trends. This fusion enables wearers to showcase their progressive mindset and embrace the best of both worlds.

7. Confidence and Empowerment: Salwar Kameez has the power to boost confidence and empower individuals. When wearing an outfit that aligns with their identity and makes them feel comfortable, individuals exude confidence and radiate self-assurance. It becomes a means of self-empowerment, allowing individuals to take on the world with grace and poise.

Salwar Kameez transcends mere clothing and becomes a tool for self-expression, empowerment, and celebration of one's individuality. It serves as a reminder that fashion is not just about aesthetics but also about personal empowerment and embracing one's unique identity. By wearing Salwar Kameez, individuals can confidently navigate the world while staying true to their cultural heritage and personal style.

Cultural Appreciation versus Appropriation

The topic of cultural appreciation versus cultural appropriation is an important consideration when discussing the adoption of cultural elements, including clothing like Salwar Kameez. Here are some key points to understand the difference between the two:

Cultural Appreciation: Cultural appreciation refers to the respectful and genuine admiration and celebration of different cultures. It involves learning about and understanding the significance, history, and context of cultural practices, including clothing, and honoring them in a way that promotes cultural understanding, inclusivity, and unity. Cultural appreciation recognizes and values the contributions of different cultures, fostering a sense of curiosity, respect, and appreciation for their traditions and heritage.

Appropriation: Cultural appropriation, on the other hand, occurs when elements of a marginalized culture are adopted, often without understanding or respect for their cultural significance, and are used for personal gain, trendiness, or without proper acknowledgment. Appropriation can be harmful as it can perpetuate stereotypes, misrepresent cultures, and strip away the cultural context, reducing significant cultural practices to mere fashion trends.

It is important to approach cultural elements, including clothing like Salwar Kameez, with sensitivity and respect. Here are some guidelines to promote cultural appreciation:

1. Educate Yourself: Take the time to learn about the cultural significance, history, and context of the attire you are interested in. Understand the meaning behind

the garments and the communities they belong to.

2. Respect and Acknowledge: When wearing cultural clothing, acknowledge its origins and give credit to the culture it represents. Avoid misrepresenting or appropriating cultural symbols and practices.

3. Avoid Stereotyping: Be conscious of any stereotypes associated with cultural attire and avoid perpetuating them. Appreciate the diversity within a culture and recognize that it is not a monolithic entity.

4. Engage in Ethical Practices: Support artisans, weavers, and designers from the respective cultural communities. Choose authentic and ethically made garments, and avoid mass-produced imitations that exploit cultural elements for profit.

5. Seek Permission: When participating in cultural events or ceremonies where traditional attire is expected, seek guidance and permission to ensure you are following appropriate customs and protocols.

6. Foster Cultural Exchange: Instead of appropriating cultural elements, strive for meaningful cultural exchange. Engage in dialogues, share knowledge, and foster understanding between cultures, promoting inclusivity and respect.

By embracing cultural appreciation and understanding, individuals can celebrate and share the beauty of cultural attire like Salwar Kameez in a respectful and responsible manner, contributing to a more inclusive and diverse society.

Handloom and Sustainable Practices

Handloom and sustainable practices play a crucial role in the production and promotion of Salwar Kameez and other traditional garments. Here are some key points to understand their significance:

1. Handloom Tradition: Handloom weaving is an age-old craft that involves weaving fabric manually using traditional looms. Handloom textiles are known for their unique textures, intricate patterns, and high-quality craftsmanship. By supporting handloom practices, we contribute to the preservation of traditional weaving techniques, empower artisans, and sustain local economies.

2. Environmental Sustainability: Handloom textiles are often produced using natural fibers such as cotton, silk, or wool, which are biodegradable and have a lower environmental impact compared to synthetic materials. Additionally, handloom weaving requires less energy and water consumption compared to large-scale mechanized production methods.

3. Empowering Artisans: Handloom weaving provides livelihood opportunities for skilled artisans, particularly in rural areas. By supporting handloom practices, we contribute to the socio-economic development of these communities and help preserve their cultural heritage.

4. Fair Trade and Ethical Practices: Emphasizing fair trade principles ensures that artisans receive fair wages, safe working conditions, and respect for their traditional

knowledge and skills. By promoting fair trade and ethical practices, we help create a more equitable and sustainable fashion industry.

5. Revival of Traditional Techniques: Handloom practices are deeply rooted in cultural traditions and techniques that have been passed down through generations. By valuing and supporting handloom textiles, we contribute to the preservation and revival of these traditional weaving techniques, ensuring their continuity for future generations.

6. Slow Fashion Movement: Handloom textiles are often associated with the principles of the slow fashion movement, which advocates for mindful consumption, durability, and a reduced environmental footprint. By choosing handloom Salwar Kameez and supporting sustainable fashion practices, we promote a more conscious and responsible approach to dressing.

7. Supporting Sustainable Brands: Look for brands and designers that prioritize sustainable and ethical practices, including the use of handloom textiles. These brands often work directly with weavers and artisans, ensuring fair wages, promoting sustainable production processes, and offering transparent supply chains.

By embracing handloom textiles and sustainable practices in the production and consumption of Salwar Kameez, we contribute to the preservation of cultural heritage, support local economies, and promote a more environmentally and socially conscious fashion industry.

Supporting Artisans and Craftsmanship

Supporting artisans and craftsmanship in the context of Salwar Kameez is crucial for the preservation of traditional skills and the livelihood of artisans. Here's why it's important:

1. Cultural Heritage Preservation: Artisans play a vital role in preserving the rich cultural heritage associated with Salwar Kameez. They possess unique skills and techniques that have been passed down through generations, contributing to the authenticity and craftsmanship of these garments. By supporting artisans, we ensure the continuity of these traditional practices.

2. Economic Empowerment: Many artisans rely on their craft for their livelihoods. By supporting them and purchasing their handmade Salwar Kameez, we contribute to their economic empowerment. This helps in sustaining their livelihoods, preserving traditional art forms, and uplifting their communities.

3. Promoting Ethical and Sustainable Practices: Artisans often employ sustainable practices in their work, such as using natural dyes, handloom weaving, and eco-friendly materials. By supporting them, we contribute to the promotion of ethical and sustainable fashion. Artisan-made Salwar Kameez embodies slow fashion principles, emphasizing quality, durability, and timeless appeal.

4. Unique and Authentic Products: Artisan-made Salwar Kameez are characterized by their intricate craftsmanship, attention to detail, and unique designs.

By choosing these garments, we have the opportunity to own and wear one-of-a-kind pieces that showcase the skill and creativity of artisans. This adds a special touch of authenticity and exclusivity to our wardrobe.

5. Cultural Exchange and Appreciation: Supporting artisans and purchasing their handmade Salwar Kameez promotes cultural exchange and appreciation. It allows us to connect with the stories, traditions, and artistry behind these garments. By wearing and sharing these pieces, we celebrate the diversity and beauty of different cultures.

6. Revival of Traditional Crafts: In recent times, traditional crafts and artisanal skills have faced challenges due to changing fashion trends and mass production. By supporting artisans, we contribute to the revival and rejuvenation of these crafts. It encourages younger generations to learn and carry forward these traditional skills, ensuring their continuity for future generations.

7. Preserving Artistic Heritage: Artisans are custodians of artistic heritage. Their craftsmanship represents the culmination of centuries-old knowledge and techniques. By supporting them, we become part of the movement to preserve and protect these valuable cultural assets, ensuring their survival for years to come.

Supporting artisans and craftsmanship in the context of Salwar Kameez is not just about owning beautiful garments but also about acknowledging the skill, dedication, and cultural significance embedded in each creation. It is a way to contribute to the sustainability, diversity, and continuity of traditional arts and crafts.

Celebrating Regional Styles and Cultural Exchange

Celebrating regional styles and promoting cultural exchange through Salwar Kameez is a wonderful way to embrace diversity, appreciate different traditions, and foster mutual understanding. Here are some reasons why it's important to celebrate regional styles and engage in cultural exchange:

1. Appreciation of Cultural Diversity: India is a land of diverse cultures, each with its unique traditions and clothing styles. By celebrating regional styles of Salwar Kameez, we embrace the richness of this cultural diversity. It allows us to explore the distinctive aesthetics, craftsmanship, and design sensibilities of different regions.

2. Showcasing Cultural Identity: Regional styles of Salwar Kameez reflect the cultural identity and heritage of specific communities and regions. By wearing and showcasing these styles, we express our respect and admiration for the traditions and values associated with them. It is a way of connecting with our roots and celebrating our own cultural identity.

3. Encouraging Cultural Exchange: Salwar Kameez is not limited to any particular region or community. It transcends boundaries and has gained popularity across the country and beyond. Embracing regional styles of Salwar Kameez encourages cultural exchange, allowing individuals from diverse backgrounds to appreciate and learn from each other's traditions.

4. Promoting Cultural Understanding: Cultural exchange through Salwar Kameez fosters mutual understanding and appreciation among different communities. By learning about and experiencing the clothing styles, customs, and aesthetics of various regions, we gain a deeper understanding of different cultures. This helps break down stereotypes, promote inclusivity, and create a more harmonious society.

5. Preserving Traditional Crafts: Celebrating regional styles of Salwar Kameez supports the preservation of traditional crafts and techniques. Each region has its unique weaving, embroidery, and printing methods that are integral to the creation of these garments. By embracing and promoting these styles, we contribute to the sustainability and continuation of these traditional crafts.

6. Bridging Generational Gaps: Regional styles of Salwar Kameez often have a rich history and are passed down through generations. By celebrating and wearing these styles, we bridge generational gaps and ensure that the knowledge and appreciation of these traditions are carried forward. It allows younger generations to connect with their cultural heritage and fosters a sense of pride and belonging.

7. Enhancing Personal Style: Exploring regional styles of Salwar Kameez offers a wealth of inspiration to enhance our personal style. Each region's unique motifs, colors, and techniques provide endless possibilities for creative expression. Incorporating elements from different regions into our wardrobe allows us to curate a truly eclectic and individualistic style.

Celebrating regional styles and engaging in cultural exchange through Salwar Kameez not only enriches our fashion choices but also deepens our understanding and appreciation of diverse cultures. It promotes inclusivity, respect, and a sense of shared humanity, creating a world where cultural diversity is celebrated and cherished.

Exploring Unique Design Elements

When it comes to Salwar Kameez, there are several unique design elements that contribute to the charm and individuality of this traditional Indian outfit. Here are some key design elements worth exploring:

1. Necklines: The neckline of a Salwar Kameez can vary greatly and adds character to the overall look. From round and V-neck to sweetheart and boat neck, there are numerous options to choose from. Each neckline has its own aesthetic appeal and can be embellished with embroidery, beading, or lacework to enhance its beauty.

2. Sleeves: The sleeves of a Salwar Kameez offer endless design possibilities. They can be long, short, or even sleeveless, depending on personal preference and occasion. Sleeves can be plain or adorned with intricate embroidery, lacework, or cuffs to add a touch of elegance and grace.

3. Hemlines: The hemline of the Kameez (tunic) can be straight, asymmetrical, or flared. Each style creates a different silhouette and visual appeal. An asymmetrical hemline adds a contemporary touch, while a flared hemline gives a more traditional and graceful look. Additionally, the use of contrasting borders or trims on the hemline adds a unique element to the design.

4. Dupatta (Scarves): The dupatta is a versatile accessory that accompanies the Salwar Kameez. It can be worn in various ways, draped over the shoulders, wrapped around the neck, or styled as a headscarf. The dupatta offers an opportunity to experiment with different

fabrics, prints, and embellishments, allowing for a personalized touch to the overall ensemble.

5. Embroidery and Embellishments: Embroidery plays a significant role in enhancing the beauty of Salwar Kameez. From intricate threadwork and mirror work to zari (metallic thread) and sequin embellishments, there are numerous embroidery techniques and embellishment options to explore. These decorative elements add texture, richness, and visual interest to the outfit.

6. Prints and Patterns: Prints and patterns are another important aspect of Salwar Kameez design. Floral prints, geometric patterns, paisley motifs, and abstract designs are commonly used. These prints can be traditional, contemporary, or a fusion of both, allowing for a wide range of creative expression.

7. Color Combinations: The choice of colors is crucial in Salwar Kameez design. Traditional color palettes, such as vibrant reds, deep blues, and earthy tones, are often favored. However, contemporary designs also incorporate a wide array of colors, including pastels, neutrals, and bold hues. The combination of colors can evoke different moods, express personal style, and create visual harmony.

8. Silhouettes and Cuts: Salwar Kameez designs offer various silhouettes and cuts to cater to different body types and style preferences. From straight-cut suits to flared Anarkali styles, from fitted churidar suits to relaxed palazzo sets, there is a design for every occasion and individual taste. The choice of silhouette can dramatically transform the overall look and impact of the outfit.

Exploring these unique design elements allows for a deeper appreciation of the artistry and creativity involved in Salwar Kameez. It offers an opportunity to experiment, customize, and create ensembles that reflect personal style and cultural aesthetics. By exploring these design elements, one can truly embrace the beauty and versatility of this traditional Indian attire.

Recap of Key Insights and Takeaways

Throughout our exploration of Salwar Kameez, we have discovered numerous key insights and takeaways. Here is a recap of the main points:

1. Salwar Kameez is a traditional Indian attire consisting of a tunic (Kameez), loose-fitting pants (Salwar), and a dupatta (scarf).
2. It holds significant cultural and historical importance, symbolizing tradition, elegance, and versatility.
3. Salwar Kameez styles vary across different regions of India, each reflecting its unique cultural influences and design elements.
4. There is a wide range of Salwar Kameez styles, including Patiala Salwar, Churidar Salwar, Palazzo Salwar, Anarkali Kameez, A-line Kameez, and more.
5. Fabrics used in Salwar Kameez range from traditional choices like cotton, silk, and chiffon to contemporary options like georgette and crepe.
6. Embroidery, embellishments, prints, and patterns play a crucial role in enhancing the beauty of Salwar Kameez, offering endless design possibilities.
7. Salwar Kameez can be styled for various occasions, including casual wear, office wear, formal events, parties, and weddings.
8. It is important to choose the right silhouette, fabric, and color combination to flatter different body types and personal preferences.
9. Accessorizing with jewelry, footwear, and dupatta draping techniques adds the finishing touch to complete

the Salwar Kameez ensemble.

10. Salwar Kameez has gained international recognition and has influenced fashion trends globally, showcasing the richness of Indian craftsmanship and design.

11. Cultural appreciation and responsible fashion practices are vital in preserving and promoting the legacy of Salwar Kameez.

12. Salwar Kameez empowers individuals to express their personal style, embrace cultural heritage, and celebrate diversity.

By understanding these key insights and takeaways, we can fully appreciate the beauty, versatility, and cultural significance of Salwar Kameez. It is an attire that bridges tradition and modernity, offering a timeless elegance that transcends boundaries and celebrates the richness of Indian fashion.

Encouragement to Embrace and Preserve Salwar Kameez

In conclusion, I would like to encourage everyone to embrace and preserve the beauty of Salwar Kameez. This traditional Indian attire is not just a garment; it is a symbol of cultural heritage, artistic craftsmanship, and personal expression. By wearing and appreciating Salwar Kameez, we not only adorn ourselves in exquisite fabrics and designs but also become ambassadors of tradition and diversity.

Whether you are of Indian descent or simply appreciate the richness of Indian fashion, incorporating Salwar Kameez into your wardrobe allows you to celebrate the beauty of different cultures and showcase your unique style. The versatility of Salwar Kameez offers endless possibilities for casual wear, formal occasions, festive celebrations, and everything in between.

By supporting artisans, weavers, and craftsmen who dedicate their skills to creating Salwar Kameez, we contribute to the preservation of traditional techniques and sustain their livelihoods. Opting for handloom fabrics, sustainable practices, and ethical fashion choices not only helps to protect the environment but also ensures that the legacy of Salwar Kameez continues for future generations to appreciate.

Let us embrace the grace, elegance, and vibrant colors of Salwar Kameez as a celebration of our cultural diversity and shared humanity. Through our choices and actions, we can ensure that this timeless attire continues to be cherished and admired for years to come. So, explore the countless styles, experiment with fusion ensembles, and let the world witness the beauty and allure of Salwar Kameez.